The Trail of Tears

CORNERSTONES OF FREEDOM

SECOND SERIES

Deborah Kent

Children's Press®
A Division of Scholastic Inc.
New York • Toronto • London • Auckland • Sydney
Mexico City • New Delhi • Hong Kong
Danbury, Connecticut

Photographs © 2005: Art Resource, NY/Smithsonian American Art
Museum, Washington, DC: 7 left; Bridgeman Art Library International
Ltd., London/New York/Kennedy Galleries, New York, USA: 10, 44
bottom left; Corbis Images: 29 (Tom Bean), 11, 37, 39, 45 top right
(Bettmann); Georgia Archives: 28 left; Gilcrease Museum, Tulsa,
Oklahoma: 9 center top, 9 bottom, 9 center bottom, 9 top;
Hulton|Archive/Getty Images: 6, 22, 44 top left (MPI), 28 right; Library of
Congress: 20, 44 bottom right; National Geographic Image Collection: 32;
Nativestock.com/Marilynn "Angel" Wynn: cover bottom, 13, 17 bottom,
27, 31, 34, 35, 40, 41; North Wind Picture Archives: 5, 7 right, 12, 14,
15, 17 top, 21 right, 21 left, 26, 44 top right, 45 bottom; Photri Inc.: 24;
Raymond Bial: 25; Robertstock.com: 19; Stock Montage, Inc.: 16, 18;
Western History Collections, Universtiy of Oklahoma Library: 3, 38;
Woolaroc Museum, Bartlesville, OK: cover top, 33, 45 ("Trail of Tears",
by Robert Lindneux).

Library of Congress Cataloging-in-Publication Data
Kent, Deborah
 The Trail of Tears / Deborah Kent.—1st ed.
  p. cm. — (Cornerstones of freedom. Second series)
 Includes bibliographical references and index.
 ISBN 0-516-23624-5
 1. Trail of Tears, 1838—Juvenile literature. 2. Five Civilized Tribes—
Relocation—Juvenile literature. 3. Cherokee Indians—Relocation—
Juvenile literature. 4. Indian Territory—History—Juvenile literature.
I. Title. II. Series.
 E99.C5K39 2005
 973.04'97557—dc22

                                            2004014455

1 2 3 4 5 6 7 8 9 10 R 14 13 12 11 10 09 08 07 06 05

IN 1828, NEW ECHOTA, THE CAPITAL of the Cherokee nation, was a thriving town with tree-lined streets and neat frame houses. Some of the Cherokee ran stores, taverns, and other businesses. Most children attended schools run by Protestant **missionaries**. The Cherokee Council planned to open an academy of higher learning. Elias Boudinot, a Cherokee who had been educated in New England, edited a newspaper called the *Cherokee Phoenix*. In the surrounding countryside, Cherokee farmers raised corn, wheat, cattle, and hogs. The men tended the livestock, while the women hoed the fields.

WORDS ON PAPER

As a Cherokee boy growing up, Sequoyah sometimes met white people who came to his village in present-day Tennessee. He was fascinated by the words they read from books and papers. Years later, Sequoyah set to work devising a writing system for the Cherokee language. Sequoyah's system used symbols to represent the syllables of Cherokee words. The system was easy to learn, and most Cherokee became **literate** after its invention in 1821.

In a number of ways, New Echota resembled the typical American town of its era. The Cherokee had adopted many of the customs and beliefs of white Americans. They had made a series of changes to survive among their white neighbors. Yet the Cherokee were determined to remain a distinct people. They held on to their native language and their ancient legends. They kept many of the traditions that had passed down through the generations.

In 1827, the Cherokee Nation ratified a constitution modeled on the Constitution of the United States. The Cherokee Constitution created a two-house **legislature** much like the U.S. Congress. The nation was headed by a principal chief. Those accused of crimes were tried in courts of law.

The Cherokee Nation, spreading over ten million acres (four million hectares) in present-day Georgia, was officially recognized by the United States in 1791. In that year, the Cherokee and the U.S. government signed an agreement called the Treaty of Holston. Under this treaty, the United States promised to respect Cherokee **sovereignty**. The Cherokee were free to make their own laws, trade agreements, and treaties. The land within their borders belonged solely to them. No outsider had the right to cross the nation's borders without Cherokee approval.

CONSTITUTION

OF THE

CHEROKEE NATION,

MADE AND ESTABLISHED

AT A

GENERAL CONVENTION OF DELEGATES,

DULY AUTHORISED FOR THAT PURPOSE.

AT

NEW ECHOTA,

JULY 26, 1827.

PRINTED FOR THE CHEROKEE NATION,
AT THE OFFICE OF THE STATESMAN AND PATRIOT,
GEORGIA.

On July 26, 1827, the first Cherokee constitution was signed into law. It was modeled after the United States Constitution.

Artist W. H. Jackson depicts white settlers arriving at a Native American camp in the West. Pioneering settlers were anxious to own land at any cost.

When the Treaty of Holston was signed, the United States was a young nation stretching along the Atlantic coast from Georgia to present-day Maine. Its people were full of plans and hopes. They hungered to push westward into the wilderness across the Appalachian Mountains. In order to expand, however, the United States had to deal with the native peoples who lived on its borders. The Cherokee and dozens of other Indian tribes had lived for thousands of years on the land where white Americans wanted to settle.

Henry Knox, who served as secretary of war under President George Washington, believed that the Indians could be **assimilated** into white society. To assimilate means to blend in and become part of a larger group. Knox was convinced that white society was superior to that of the Native Americans. Yet he felt that the Indians were capable of becoming "civilized" if given the proper opportunity. The Treaty of Holston stated that, "the Cherokee Nation may be led to a greater degree of civilization, with [its people] becoming herdsmen and cultivators [farmers] instead of remaining in a state of hunters." Just as Knox predicted, the Cherokee embraced many features of American society. At the same time, however, they kept a strong hold on their Cherokee **identity**. They saw themselves as a strong, proud people adapting to a changing world.

Henry Knox believed that whites were superior to Native Americans. He felt the United States government could change the Indians' culture to be more "civilized."

George Catlin was well known for his paintings of Native Americans. This painting is called *Pigeon's Egg Head*, and it shows an American Indian before and after contact with whites.

THE INDIANS OF THE SOUTHEAST

Early in the 1600s, Europeans reached the region which is now the southeastern United States. At that time, the Cherokee lived in a wide area that included parts of North Carolina, South Carolina, Georgia, Kentucky, Tennessee, Alabama, and West Virginia. The Cherokee were divided into seven kinship groups or **clans**. Most clans were named for animals such as the bear, deer, or wolf. The members of each clan were deeply loyal to one another.

This map shows the original Cherokee homeland, covering parts of Kentucky, Tennessee, West Virginia, North Carolina, South Carolina, Georgia, and Alabama.

The Cherokee lived by hunting and farming. The women raised corn, beans, squash, and other crops. The men hunted game such as deer, rabbits, and ducks. Decisions affecting the clan were made after discussions in a building called the Great Council House. In these discussions, both women and men were free to speak.

Cherokee families traced their ancestry through the female line. When a man married, he moved into his wife's household. The child of a Cherokee mother was considered a Cherokee, regardless of the father's **heritage**. Thus the son of a Cherokee mother and a white father was fully accepted as a member of the Cherokee tribe.

Several other American Indian tribes also lived in the Southeast. The Creek occupied eastern Alabama. In northern Mississippi lived the Chickasaw, and to the south lived their close neighbors, the Choctaw. Later, another Indian group, the Seminole, settled in the swamps and marshes of present-day Florida.

The Seminoles were not a distinct tribe with a common language and customs. They were, instead, people from several tribes who fled to the swamps as white settlers moved onto their land. Runaway African American slaves sometimes joined the Seminole bands.

Shown here are important members of four of the "Five Civilized Tribes"—Seminole chief Chittee Yoholo, Choctaw warrior Push-Ma-Ta-Ha, Creek chief McIntosh, and Cherokee chief David Vann.

Native Americans watch a wagon train of white settlers make its way west.

★ ★ ★ ★

THE COMING OF THE UNAKAS

During the 1600s, white traders and settlers trickled into the present-day southeastern states. Soon the trickle of whites swelled to a steady stream. The Cherokee called the newcomers *unakas*, meaning "white-skinned strangers."

The Europeans brought trade goods that the Indians had never seen before: iron kettles and ax blades, gunpowder, and rum. The Indians traded furs and deerskins to acquire these goods. The Europeans also brought a host of diseases to which the Indians had never been exposed. **Epidemics**

10

of smallpox, measles, and other illnesses swept from one village to another. Historians believe that the Cherokee numbered about thirty thousand before they met Europeans early in the 1600s. By 1700, the Cherokee population was cut almost in half, reduced by disease to about sixteen thousand. Neighboring tribes were also devastated.

From the beginning, white settlers were eager to seize the Indians' land. The Indians resisted bravely, but they were

During colonial times, Native Americans traded furs in exchange for European goods such as guns, gunpowder, and ax blades.

severely weakened by the deadly epidemics. The whites arrived in ever-increasing numbers. It seemed that nothing could stop them. During the American Revolution (1776–1783), the Cherokee sided with the British, who promised to protect their lands from the colonists. The colonists burned Indian villages and killed men, women, and children on sight. The legislature of South Carolina even offered rewards, or bounties, for Indian scalps. One Cherokee band, the Chickamauga, continued to fight fiercely in Tennessee until 1794. Most of the Indians, however, withdrew deeper into the forests, hoping they could escape their tormentors. By the end of the revolution, the Indians had lost some 9,800 square miles (2,500 km) of territory.

A British general talks with Native Americans to create an alliance, or team, against the colonists during the American Revolution.

During the Creek War, the Creeks fought against the Americans as well as some Indian tribes, including the Cherokee, the Choctaw, and the Chickasaw.

In 1813, war broke out between the Creeks and the white settlers. The Cherokee sided with the whites in the conflict. One of the white leaders in the Creek War was a fiery young army officer named Andrew Jackson, who grew up on the frontier. Like most settlers, he believed that Indians were inferior to whites and that whites should take over all Indian lands east of the Mississippi River. Andrew Jackson was destined to play a key role in the story of the Cherokee Nation.

OLD HICKORY

Orphaned at fourteen, Andrew Jackson grew up on the North Carolina frontier. Later, he moved to Tennessee, where he became a lawyer and entered politics. Jackson led successful military campaigns in the Creek War and the War of 1812. Because of his toughness, he earned the nickname Old Hickory. In 1828, Jackson became the seventh president of the United States. He is remembered for his motto, "To the victor go the spoils."

13

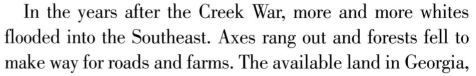

In the early 1800s, whites began to claim even more land in the Southeast. Here, white settlers clear a plot of land and prepare to build a fence around their homes.

In the years after the Creek War, more and more whites flooded into the Southeast. Axes rang out and forests fell to make way for roads and farms. The available land in Georgia, the Carolinas, Tennessee, and Alabama filled quickly. The settlers eyed the Indian lands more greedily than ever. They began to speak openly about "Indian removal." The Indians, they said, should be sent west of the Mississippi to make room for white expansion. The U.S. government set aside land in present-day Oklahoma, hoping that the southeastern tribes could be persuaded to settle there.

As early as 1810, some Cherokee and other southeastern Indians sold their land to white farmers and headed west. But most of the Indians wanted to stay on the land that had been their home for generations. They did not want to leave their fertile farmland and the graves of their ancestors. To stop members of the tribe from giving up more territory, the Cherokee Legislature passed a law against selling land to whites. The crime of selling land could be punished by death.

Some Indian tribes quietly migrated to the West as whites took over more of their land.

DECISIONS IN WASHINGTON

In November 1828, Andrew Jackson was elected president of the United States. The Cherokee had helped Jackson during the Creek War. According to one story, Cherokee warriors even saved Jackson's life during an ambush. Nevertheless, Jackson had no personal loyalty to the Cherokee. To him, all Indians were basically alike, and

General Andrew Jackson led American forces during the Creek War. He is shown here accepting the surrender of a Creek chief.

they could never be equal to whites. Jackson stood by his conviction that the land east of the Mississippi should be entirely under white control. In land disputes between the state of Georgia and the Cherokee Nation, Jackson sided with Georgia.

When flecks of gold were discovered near the Cherokee town of Dahlonega in 1829, gold-hungry whites rushed onto Cherokee land. They stole Indian cattle, terrorized Indian women, and started fights with Indian men. Many of the

* * * *

younger Cherokee wanted to put up armed resistance. Older members of the tribe warned that violence would only lead to more trouble. An article in the *Cherokee Phoenix* stated, "It has been the desire of our enemies that the Cherokee may be urged to some desperate act. Thus far, this desire has never been realized, and we hope . . . this **forbearance** will continue." Rather than fight, Cherokee leaders counseled that the tribe ask for help from the U.S. government in Washington, D.C. With Jackson in the White House, however, the Cherokee found little support.

Late in 1829, a proposed law, or bill, came before the U.S. Congress for consideration. The bill was called the Indian Removal Act.

Miners search for gold in Dahlonega, Georgia.

The *Cherokee Phoenix* was the first Native American newspaper in the United States. Its editorials often discussed Cherokee concerns, such as the relationship with the U.S. government and their efforts to regain land.

It called for the forced removal of some one hundred thousand eastern Indians to the Oklahoma Territory. The Indians' land would then be made available to white settlers. President Jackson gave the bill his unquestioning approval. He argued that removal would actually benefit the Indians. In the West, they would find a safe haven where they could start fresh. In his State of the Union address in 1830, Jackson further justified the legislation.

> *Doubtless it will be painful [for the Indians] to leave the graves of their fathers, but what do they do more than our ancestors did, and our children are now doing? To better their condition in an unknown land our forefathers left all that was dear. . . . Our children by thousands leave yearly the land of their*

As president, Andrew Jackson did not have good relations with Native Americans. He passed the Indian Removal Act just one year after taking office.

birth to seek new homes in distant regions. . . . Can it be cruel in this government when, by events which it cannot control, the Indian is made discontented in his ancient home, to purchase his lands, to give him a new and extensive territory, to pay the expense of his removal, and to support him for a year in his new abode?

Jackson ignored the fact that whites were moving westward by choice, of their own free will. The Indian Removal Act would force the Indians to leave their homeland, in complete disregard of their wishes.

Some whites passionately opposed the Indian Removal Act. Protestant missionaries who had lived and worked among the Indians championed their rights to the land. In a piece for the *Washington Intelligencer*, a missionary named Jeremiah Evarts reminded his readers that George Washington himself had signed the treaty that recognized the Cherokee Nation. The original treaty had been upheld by several other agreements over the next four decades. "Is the Senate of the United States . . . to march in solemn procession, and burn a whole volume of treaties?" Evarts demanded. "When ambassadors from foreign nations inquire, 'What is the cause of all this burning?' are we to say, . . . 'The treaties are plain, and the terms reasonable. But the Indians are weak, and their white neighbors will be lawless. The way to please these white neighbors is, therefore, to

George Washington signed a treaty that created the Cherokee Nation [1791].

21st CONGRESS.
1st Session.

S. 102.

IN SENATE OF THE UNITED STATES.

FEBRUARY 22, 1830.

Mr. WHITE, from the Committee on Indian Affairs, reported the following bill; which was read, and passed to a second reading:

A BILL

To provide for an exchange of lands with the Indians residing in any of the States or Territories, and for their removal West of the river Mississippi.

1   *Be it enacted by the Senate and House of Representatives*
2   *of the United States of America in Congress assembled,* That
3   it shall and may be lawful for the President of the Unit-
4   ed States to cause so much of any territory belonging to the Unit-
5   ed States, West of the river Mississippi, not included in any
6   State, and to which the Indian title has been extinguished, as
7   he may judge necessary, to be divided into a suitable number
8   of districts, for the reception of such tribes or nations of Indi-
9   ans as may choose to exchange the lands where they now re-
10   side, and remove there; and to cause each of said districts to
11   be so described by natural or artificial marks, as to be easily
12   distinguished from every other.

1   SEC. 2. *And be it further enacted,* That it shall and may
2   be lawful for the President to exchange any or all of such
3   districts, so to be laid off and described, with any tribe or na-
4   tion of Indians now residing, within the limits of any of the

This bill for Indian removal was presented to the Senate on February 22, 1830. The senators hotly debated the bill before the final vote was passed in its favor.

burn the treaties, and then call the Indians our dear children, and deal with them precisely as if no treaties had ever been made.'"

Despite such protests, the Indian Removal Act was signed into law on May 28, 1830. Whites on the frontier celebrated the news, while the Indians reeled in shock. They could scarcely believe that the lawmakers in Washington had betrayed them. Many white Americans, especially in the Northeast, were outraged by the act. Massachusetts representative Edward Everett stated, "The evil is enormous, the inevitable suffering incalculable. . . . We ourselves, when the interests and passions of the day are past, shall look back upon it, I fear, with self-reproach and a regret both bitter and **unavailing**."

With the Indian Removal Act in place, the state of Georgia began to parcel out Cherokee land to its white citizens. The Cherokee protested this treatment and appealed to state and federal officials. Eventually, they took their case to the U.S. Supreme Court. The court's decision, handed down in 1832, seemed to challenge the Indian Removal Act. Chief Justice John Marshall ruled that, "the Cherokee Nation is a distinct community, occupying its own territory with boundaries accurately described, and which the citizens of Georgia have no right to enter but with the **assent** of the Cherokees themselves."

20

The Cherokee rejoiced. At last, the powerful men in Washington were upholding the rights of the Cherokee. Surely the Court's decision meant that they could keep their land after all. But President Jackson was not ready to back down. "John Marshall has rendered his decision," he said. "Now let him enforce it." The president, or chief executive of the United States, was responsible for enforcing court decisions. President Jackson refused to support a decision that opposed the Indian Removal Act.

This is the title page of the U.S. Supreme Court record for the *Cherokee Nation v. State of Georgia*, 1831 (below left). Chief Justice John Marshall (below right) ruled in favor of the Cherokee, but his decision would ultimately have little effect.

THE CASE

OF

THE CHEROKEE NATION

against

THE STATE OF GEORGIA:

ARGUED AND DETERMINED AT

THE SUPREME COURT OF THE UNITED STATES,

JANUARY TERM 1831.

WITH

AN APPENDIX,

Containing the Opinion of Chancellor Kent on the Case; the Treaties between the United States and the Cherokee Indians; the Act of Congress of 1802, entitled ' An Act to regulate intercourse with the Indian tribes, &c.'; and the Laws of Georgia relative to the country occupied by the Cherokee Indians, within the boundary of that State.

BY RICHARD PETERS,

COUNSELLOR AT LAW.

Philadelphia:

JOHN GRIGG, 9 NORTH FOURTH STREET.

1831.

PARTING FROM THE LAND

On an autumn morning in 1831, a group of Choctaw women walked among the trees outside their village. With tears in their eyes, they touched the leaves and branches. They stroked the bark as if they wanted to commit each knot and crevice to memory. At last, they returned to the village. U.S. Army troops waited to escort the villagers to Vicksburg, Mississippi.

By December 1831, some four thousand Choctaws were packed into log forts, or stockades, in Vicksburg, waiting to begin their sad journey west. They had been forced to leave most of their belongings behind. "They are generally very naked, and few moccasins are seen among them," wrote one

This painting shows a Choctaw Indian encampment on the Mississippi River around 1833.

of the agents in charge of the removal. "If I could have done it with propriety, I would have given them shoes." The government had promised to supply the Indians with food, blankets, and clothing for the trip to Oklahoma. Few provisions ever appeared. Hungry, cold, and deeply discouraged, the Choctaws set off toward an unknown land. Hundreds died of smallpox and dysentery along the way. "Death was always among us," an agent wrote, "and the road was lined with the sick. The extra wagons hired to haul the sick are about five to the thousand. Fortunately they are a people that will walk to the last, or I do not know how we could get on."

The Creek removal began in 1836, after a handful of Indians clashed with militia in Georgia and Alabama. The militia used these small battles, or skirmishes, as an excuse to drive the Creeks from their homes. Those who resisted were put in chains. Some Creeks escaped and joined the Seminole bands in Florida. Most were herded westward. As they marched toward Oklahoma, the Creeks sang a mournful song:

> *I have no more land,*
> *I am driven away from home,*
> *Driven up the red waters.*
> *Let us all go.*
> *Let us all die together.*

The next tribe to face removal was the Chickasaw. Many of the Chickasaw paid their own expenses on the westward journey rather than depending on the military to provide food and clothing. They raised money by selling their land

23

The Chickasaw were also forced to move west. They eventually founded a new settlement in Oklahoma alongside the Choctaw.

to eager white farmers. Riding their own horses, they traveled at a pace they set themselves. Other Chickasaw, however, refused to sell their land. Soldiers with guns and bayonets finally forced them to leave. As they trudged along or rode in military wagons, the Chickasaw put up a silent resistance. One agent complained, "[They] seem to take great satisfaction in disregarding all directions and orders they receive from us."

Among the southeastern Indians, only the Seminoles turned to armed resistance. When the government announced that Seminole removal would begin early in 1836, the Indians went to war. The Seminole knew every inch of the swamps and forests where they

NEVER GIVE IN!

Despite the tireless efforts of the whites, some Indians never left the southeastern states. After the Seminole War, a few hundred Seminoles remained hidden in the Florida swamps. Several hundred Choctaws managed to escape removal by taking refuge in Mississippi's deepest forests. About one thousand Cherokee avoided being sent west and continued to live in North Carolina, Tennessee, Georgia, and Alabama. Their descendants form the group known today as the Eastern Band of the Cherokee Indians (EBCI).

After the war, some Seminole hid in the Florida swamps.

During the Seminole War, Native Americans attacked Fort King and surprised U.S. Army forces.

made their home. From their hiding places in the marshes and thickets, they made lightning strikes at the pursuing white soldiers. The Seminole War cost the federal government some forty million dollars, and fifteen hundred U.S. troops lost their lives in the fighting. In 1838, General Thomas Jessup wrote to the secretary of war, "We have committed the error of attempting to remove them when their lands were not required for agricultural purposes, when they were not in the way of the white inhabitants, and when the greater portion of their country was an unexplored wilderness." Many whites, however, deeply resented the Seminoles for sheltering runaway slaves. They were determined to drive the Seminoles westward. The Seminole War dragged on until 1843. By that time, most of the Seminoles had been rounded up and marched off to Oklahoma.

A NATION DIVIDED

The most organized of the five southeastern tribes, the Cherokee tried to bargain, or **negotiate**, with the federal government. One group, or **delegation**, after another went to Washington to speak with government officials. Though hostile whites pressed in on all sides, most Cherokee wanted to hold on to their land. John Ross, principal chief of the Cherokee Nation, expressed his people's wishes in Washington.

A few Cherokee felt that resistance of any kind was hopeless. They believed that the Cherokee should sell their land and move west. In the pages of the *Cherokee Phoenix*,

As leader of the Cherokee Nation, John Ross is remembered for his role in fighting against the removal of his people.

Elias Boudinot (left) and John Ridge (right) felt that the Cherokee should negotiate with the U.S. government.

Elias Boudinot urged the Cherokee to make a treaty with the whites and accept land in Oklahoma. Boudinot and his uncle, John Ridge, led the Treaty Party, a small but vocal group that launched its own negotiations with Washington.

John Ross was outraged by the actions of the Treaty Party. He felt that Ridge, Boudinot, and their followers did not represent the Cherokee majority. They had no right to speak for the Cherokee people. Ross forced Boudinot to resign as

★ ★ ★ ★

editor of the *Cherokee Phoenix*. Ridge was removed from his seat on the tribal council. Yet the Treaty Party could not be silenced. In the fall of 1835, while John Ross was busy in Washington, John Ridge signed a treaty with government officials at the Cherokee capital, New Echota. Under the Treaty of New Echota, the Cherokee gave up all of their land east of the Mississippi. In return, they would receive five million dollars and a tract of land in northeastern Oklahoma. The U.S. government promised to provide the Cherokee with transportation west and financial support for their first year in the new territory. John Ridge knew that most of the Cherokee would be dismayed by these terms. He commented, "In signing this treaty I have signed my own death warrant."

The land in Oklahoma that was given to the Indians was not good for raising crops or for hunting animals. As a result, the Indians had to rely on the U.S. government for survival.

The U.S. government and the people of Georgia were delighted with the Treaty of New Echota. But as Ridge expected, most Cherokee were horrified. More than fifteen thousand Cherokee signed a letter of protest to the U.S. Congress. Despite this massive outcry, Congress ratified the treaty in 1836. Within two years, the Cherokee would have to leave their fields, their woodlands, and their homes.

THE TRAIL OF TEARS

"The Cherokees are nearly all prisoners," wrote Evan Jones, a Protestant missionary, in June 1838. "They have been dragged from their houses and encamped at the forts of military posts. . . . Multitudes were allowed no time to take anything with them except the clothes they had on. . . . Many of the Cherokees who, a few days ago, were in comfortable circumstances, are now victims of abject poverty. . . . They are prisoners without a crime to justify the fact."

For eight years, ever since Andrew Jackson signed the Indian Removal Act, the Cherokee had struggled to keep their nation together. Though about five thousand moved west of their own accord, most had stayed on their land. In the spring of 1838, the Cherokee planted their crops as usual, convinced that the Removal Act would not be enforced against them. They were wholly unprepared when their time finally ran out.

Nearly a century later, a Cherokee woman named Rebecca Neugin recalled the events of May 18, 1838, the fateful day her family was forced to move: "When the soldiers came to

The Cherokee were forced to leave behind their belongings and their homes in New Echota. This Cherokee home still stands there today as part of the New Echota Historic Site.

our house my father wanted to fight, but my mother told him that the soldiers would kill us if he did, so we surrendered. They drove us out of our house to join other prisoners in the stockade." As soon as the Cherokee were forced from their homes, white civilians rushed in to seize anything of value that was left behind. They snatched up cooking pots, tools, and even children's toys. They led away the Indians' cattle, pigs, and other livestock. Some looters even dug up Indian graves, searching for jewelry that might have been buried with the dead.

The summer of 1838 was especially hot and dry. The Cherokee were crammed into stockades without adequate food, water, or toilet facilities. Hungry and depressed, they fell easy prey to dysentery and other diseases. Hundreds died before the long westward journey even began.

The first three Cherokee groups, or **detachments**, set off for Oklahoma in June 1838, under the command of General Winfield Scott. By August, the relocation was fully under way, with nearly sixteen thousand Cherokee on the move. Supplies were scarce, disease was widespread, and the Cherokee were shattered in spirit. About

This map shows the many routes the Cherokee traveled to reach Oklahoma.

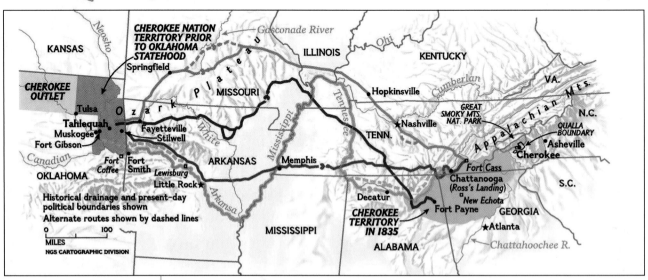

* * * *

twenty-five hundred died on the trek to Oklahoma. In the Cherokee language, this tragic journey is remembered as *Nunahi-Duna-Dlo-Hilu-I*, or "Trail Where They Cried." In English, it has come to be called the Trail of Tears.

"One can never forget the sadness and solemnity of that morning," wrote Private John G. Burnett, a young soldier who witnessed the departure of a Cherokee detachment in August 1838. "Chief John Ross led in prayer and when the bugle sounded and the wagons started rolling many of the children rose to their feet and waved their little hands good-bye to their mountain homes, knowing they were

This painting by Robert Lindneux shows the Cherokee on the Trail of Tears.

leaving them forever. Many of these helpless people did not have blankets and many of them had been driven from home barefooted."

Most of the Cherokee detachments traveled overland—in wagons, on horseback, or on foot. Covering about ten miles (16 km) a day, they camped at nightfall. The more fortunate families— those who had managed to keep a gun or bow and arrows—added game to the meager ration of oats and corn handed out by the Indian agents. Often, those who had a little extra food shared it with their hungry neighbors.

During the summer, the Cherokee traveled under a searing sun. The cooler days of autumn came as a relief, only to be followed by the winter, with its lashing winds and relentless cold. A white traveler who passed a Cherokee

*   *   *   *

With few blankets and little clothing, many Cherokee did not survive the trail in winter.

RIDING THE RIVERS

About three thousand Cherokee traveled chiefly on riverboats provided by the government. The noise of the steam-powered engines and the strange motion of the boats terrified the Indians. From three to five people a day died aboard ship, and their bodies were lowered into the river. Proper burial in the earth was important to the Cherokee. They were horrified whenever the body of a friend or relative slipped out of sight beneath the water.

detachment wrote, "Aging females, apparently nearly ready to drop into the grave, were traveling with heavy burdens attached to their backs—on the frozen ground with no covering for their feet except what nature had given them.

We learned . . . that they buried fourteen or fifteen at each stopping place."

The journey from Georgia to northeastern Oklahoma covered nearly one thousand miles (1600 km), and took each band of travelers from six to eight months. By the spring of 1839, the last ragged bands of Cherokee reached their final destination.

A NEW BEGINNING IN A NEW LAND

The woes of the Cherokee and other southeastern Indians did not end when they arrived in Oklahoma. The Cherokee who had traveled on the Trail of Tears joined about five thousand other Cherokee who had already settled on the land. Some had been there for decades and resented the newcomers. Tension between the groups nearly flared into a civil war. Eventually, the Cherokee managed to set aside their differences and write a new constitution. John Ross was reelected to serve as principal chief. Little by little, the Cherokee built a new nation, with its capital at Tahlequah, Oklahoma. Tahlequah remains the tribal headquarters of the Cherokee Nation to this day.

Like the Cherokee, the other transplanted tribes slowly gained a footing in their new land. The Creek raised hogs and cattle. The Choctaw and Chickasaw became successful farmers, raising corn for sale to nearby army posts. Missionaries complained that they refused to plant in the "proper" way, with straight, even rows, and insisted

The official seal of the Cherokee Nation was created in 1839, the same year the new constitution was adopted in Oklahoma.

on planting corn "not secured by any fence, and the land not plowed, but dug up with hoes, and planted without rows or in any order." Even in Oklahoma, the Indians held fast to ways that had served them for centuries.

The federal government promised the Indians that the new land would belong to them "for as long as the grass

A Choctaw family stands outside their log home.

grows and the waters run." Once again, however, the government set its promises aside. In the years after the U.S. Civil War (1861–1865), white settlers pushed onto Indian land in growing numbers. The federal government did little to stop them. Gradually, the Indian land was chipped away. In 1907, the region called Indian Territory was admitted to the Union as Oklahoma, the forty-sixth state.

DEATH TO THE TRAITORS

On June 22, 1839, at separate locations, John Ridge and Elias Boudinot were both executed. They had crafted the Treaty of New Echota, and many Cherokee blamed them for the disastrous Trail of Tears. Just as John Ridge predicted, the signing of the treaty sealed his death.

White settlers prepare to take part in the Oklahoma land rush in 1889.

For the most part, the Indians of Oklahoma assimilated into mainstream American society. Yet many still sense the pain of uprooting, or dispossession. The sorrow of the Trail of Tears has been carried down through the generations. Linda Hogan, a writer of Chickasaw descent, expressed the

Cherokee schoolchildren pose in front of a school in Indian Territory.

Today, American Indians continue to honor their culture and heritage as an important part of United States history. Here, Native American dancers celebrate at the capitol building in Oklahoma.

pain of this heritage: "I had an unnamed grief, not only my own. . . . There was never a language to say it, to form a geography or history or map of what had happened, not only in terms of history, but to ourselves."

Glossary

assent—approval

assimilate—to blend into another group or culture

clan—a group based on kinship ties

delegation—a group representing many citizens, sent to represent them at a meeting

detachment—on the Trail of Tears, groups of Indians forced to move from their home in the East to the land set aside in Oklahoma

epidemic—a major outbreak of disease

forbearance—holding back with patience

heritage—ethnic background

identity—sense of self

legislature—a lawmaking body of government

literate—able to read and write

missionary—a person who teaches others about religion
in an attempt to convert them

negotiate—to seek an agreement through discussion
and bargaining

sovereignty—independence as a nation

unavailing—useless; of no help

Timeline: The Trail

1791	1810	1813	1821	1827	1828	1830

| | Some southeastern Indians sell their land to whites and move west. | The Creek War breaks out between white settlers and the Creek Indians. | | | Andrew Jackson is elected president of the United States; gold is discovered on Cherokee land. | Congress passes the Indian Removal Act, calling for one hundred thousand Indians to be transported west of the Mississippi River from their homes in the East. |

CONSTITUTION

OF THE

CHEROKEE NATION,

MADE AND ESTABLISHED

AT A

GENERAL CONVENTION OF DELEGATES,

DULY AUTHORIZED FOR THAT PURPOSE.

AT

NEW ECHOTA,

JULY 26, 1827.

PRINTED FOR THE CHEROKEE NATION,
AT THE OFFICE OF THE STATESMAN AND PATRIOT,
GEORGIA.

With the Treaty of Holston, the U.S. government officially recognizes the Cherokee Nation, covering ten million acres (four million hectares) of land in present-day Georgia.

Sequoyah completes his writing system for the Cherokee language.

The Cherokee Nation ratifies a constitution creating a court system and a two-house legislature.

S. 102.

IN SENATE OF THE UNITED STATES,
FEBRUARY 22, 1830.

Mr. White, from the Committee on Indian Affairs, reported the following bill; which was read, and passed to a second reading:

A BILL

To provide for an exchange of lands with the Indians residing in any of the States or Territories, and for their removal West of the river Mississippi.

Be it enacted by the Senate and House of Representatives of the United States of America in Congress assembled, That it shall and may be lawful for the President of the United States to cause so much of any territory belonging to the United States, West of the river Mississippi, not included in any State, and to which the Indian title has been extinguished, as he may judge necessary, to be divided into a suitable number of districts, for the reception of such tribes or nations of Indians as may choose to exchange the lands where they now reside, and remove there; and to cause each of said districts to be so described by natural or artificial marks, as to be easily distinguished from every other.

Sec. 2. *And be it further enacted,* That it shall and may be lawful for the President to exchange any or all of such districts, so to be laid off and described, with any tribe or nation of Indians now residing within the limits of any of the

# of Tears

| 1831 | 1832 | 1835 | 1836 | 1838–1839 | 1843 | 1993 |

The Seminoles resist removal, beginning the Seminole War; the removal of the Creeks begins.

The Cherokees are forcibly removed to Oklahoma; their journey of one thousand miles (1,600-km) is known as the Trail of Tears.

The Seminole War ends, and most of the Seminoles are sent to Oklahoma.

The Trail of Tears Association is formed to research and commemorate the Trail of Tears.

The Choctaw are removed from Mississippi to Oklahoma.

The U.S. Supreme Court rules that the Cherokee Nation is a sovereign nation and that outsiders cannot enter without the permission of the Cherokee.

A small group of Cherokee signs the Treaty of New Echota, giving up land in the Cherokee Nation and accepting new land in present-day Oklahoma.

To Find Out More

BOOKS

Bealer, Alex W. *Only the Names Remain: The Cherokees and the Trail of Tears*. Boston: Little, Brown, 1996.

Bruchac, Joseph. *The Journal of Jesse Smoke, a Cherokee Boy: The Trail of Tears, 1838*. New York: Scholastic, 2002.

Claro, Nicole. *The Cherokee Indians*. Langhorne, PA: Chelsea House, 1993.

Elish, Dan. *The Cherokee Removal: The Story of the Trail of Tears*. Tarrytown, NY: Benchmark Books, 2002.

Fischer, Laura. *Life on the Trail of Tears*. Chicago: Heinemann, 2003.

Rozema, Vicki, ed. *Voices from the Trail of Tears*. Winston-Salem, NC: J. F. Blair, 2003.

ONLINE SITES

The Cherokee Nation: Official Site
www.cherokee.org/

Cherokee Trail of Tears Commemorative Park
www.trailoftears.org

Trail of Tears: National Historic Trail
www.arch.dcr.state.nc.us/tears

Index

Bold numbers indicate illustrations.

About the Author

Deborah Kent grew up in Little Falls, New Jersey, and received a bachelor's degree in English from Oberlin College. She earned a master's degree from Smith College School for Social Work and worked for four years at the University Settlement House in New York City. She wrote her first young-adult novel, *Belonging*, while living in the town of San Miguel de Allende in Mexico.

Ms. Kent is the author of more than a dozen novels and numerous nonfiction titles for young readers. She lives in Chicago, Illinois, with her husband, children's author R. Conrad Stein, and their daughter, Janna.